THE CBT TOOLBOX

How to Cope with your Social Anxiety, Low Self-Esteem and Negative Thoughts using CBT

by Jeremy Crown

© **Copyright 2018 - All rights reserved.**

The content contained within this book may not be reproduced, duplicated or transmitted without direct written permission from the author or the publisher.

Under no circumstances will any blame or legal responsibility be held against the publisher, or author, for any damages, reparation, or monetary loss due to the information contained within this book. Either directly or indirectly.

Legal Notice:

This book is copyright protected. This book is only for personal use. You cannot amend, distribute, sell, use, quote or paraphrase any part, or the content within this book, without the consent of the author or publisher.

Disclaimer Notice:

Please note the information contained within this document is for educational and entertainment purposes only. All effort has been executed to present accurate, up to date, and reliable, complete information. No warranties of any kind are declared or implied. Readers acknowledge that the author is not engaging in the rendering of legal, financial, medical or professional advice. The content within this book has been derived from various sources. Please consult a licensed professional before attempting any techniques outlined in this book.

By reading this document, the reader agrees that under no circumstances is the author responsible for any losses, direct or indirect, which are incurred as a result of the use of information contained within this document, including, but not limited to, — errors, omissions, or inaccuracies.

Table Of Contents

Table Of Contents 3
Introduction 7
    How to Use this Book 9
    How to Set Goals for Using CBT Tools and How to Maintain the Progress (Bonus content) 10
Chapter 1: Cognitive Behavior Therapy 11
    Understanding Cognitive Behavior Therapy 12
    Do You Need CBT? 12
    What Disorders Can CBT Treat? 13
    How CBT Works 14
    Choosing Your Therapist 15
    CBT Sessions 16
    Types of Cognitive Behavior Therapy 17
    Composition of Cognitive Behavior Therapy 19
    Lessons from CBT 20
    What if CBT Fails? 21
    Risks Associated with CBT 21
Chapter 2: Worry 23

Understanding Worry and Anxiety 24
CBT for Worry and Anxiety 25
Exposure Therapy for Anxiety 27
Managing Anxiety through CBT 29
CBT Toolbox 31

Chapter 3: Shyness and Social Anxiety *39*

Shyness 40
Understanding Social Anxiety 41
What Causes Social Anxiety? 42
Diagnosing Social Anxiety 43
CBT Toolbox 45

Chapter 4: Negative Self-Talk *51*

Understanding Negative Self-Talk 52
CBT Procedure for Negative Self-Talk 54
Positivity vs. Realism 56
CBT Toolbox 57

Chapter 5: Low Self-Esteem *63*

Understanding Low Self-Esteem 64
Using CBT for Low Self-Esteem 65
Building Self-Esteem 66
CBT Toolbox 70

Chapter 6: Low Confidence *75*

Understanding Low Confidence 76
CBT Interventions for Low Confidence 76
CBT Exercises for Low Confidence 78
CBT Toolbox 82

Chapter 7: Dealing with Depression 87
Understanding Depression 88
How Does CBT Help with Depression? 88
CBT Techniques for Depression 89
Dealing with Negative Thoughts 90
CBT Toolbox 93

Chapter 8: Improving Ineffective Communication Skills 99
Understanding Ineffective Communication Skills 100
Psychology of Listening 101
Improving Your Communication Skills 102
CBT Toolbox 105

Conclusion 111

One last thing 113

Introduction

Behavioral changes define the way you interact with people, the way you go about your life and so many things about you that you might not know yet. Mental health is getting more attention today, and that is a good thing. There are traits you portray that can be identified at an early stage and dealt with accordingly.

Cognitive Behavior Therapy (CBT) is a short-term form of treatment that will help you overcome most of your fears. These are weaknesses that might keep you away from interacting with your peers. Many people struggle with esteem issues, anxiety, depression, worry, and so forth, which might not be easy to discuss with people.

Unfortunately, most people experience these problems without even knowing it. They realize it too late when the problem has become a part of who they are. A negative thought process can do so much damage and make you feel unworthy of attention. Everyone deserves a chance. You deserve a chance. But before you expect someone else to give you a chance, why not give yourself a chance?

Things like negative self-talk hold you back. You criticize yourself so much that you believe the bad things you tell yourself. If you cannot see yourself in a good way, no one else will.

CBT is about helping you embody the change you want people to see in you. It will help you become a better version of yourself and be more confident in your ability to tackle anything that comes your way.

CBT is a method of treatment that helps patients struggling with a variety of psychological problems. To succeed in treatment, the patient and the therapist must establish a level of trust and understanding. CBT is like working with your gym trainer. You are working towards achieving certain goals.

CBT is popular today because it is a process where the patient is an active participant in the healing process. By the time you are healing, you can acknowledge the effort you put into the process. You can identify how far you have come, and appreciate the fact that you are doing better than you were at the beginning.

While it is good to focus on the awesomeness of CBT, it is also healthy to recognize that things will not always work out as they should. You might encounter disappointing experiences from time to time, and you must accept them for what they are—bumps on the road. They should never hold you back.

You will learn a lot in this book about the way negative thoughts manifest, how you allow them to creep in, and the disastrous effect this can have. You will also learn how to identify these thoughts, what to do about them, and how to overcome the challenges you encounter.

While CBT might be a short-term process, the path to recovery demands your full attention. You must be dedicated and committed to seeing this through. At the end of your therapy sessions, you should be a well-rounded individual, ready to take advantage of the opportunities that come your way. You will also see an improvement in your quality of life.

How to Use this Book

As you read this book, you will find common behavioral challenges that have been discussed which you might relate to. You will have a better understanding of the behavioral challenges you might be struggling through.

At the end of each chapter, there is a CBT Toolbox with simple exercises that you can perform from time to time. These exercises will increase your awareness of the problem you have, help you identify the triggers, and learn how to overcome it.

There is a lot of literature that has been written not just on CBT, but on the individual behavioral concerns that have been tackled in this book. However, most of these are written in a technical tone, making it difficult for most patients to comprehend.

This book has simplified the CBT approaches, and even on your own, you should be able to make significant progress towards your healing.

How to Set Goals for Using CBT Tools and How to Maintain the Progress (Bonus content)

Having effective tools and techniques is very important, although in the long term it is also critical to have clear and achievable goals to aim for.

Have you ever felt like you're moving forward and you're unstoppable, but then, suddenly, something changed and you lost your momentum? It was probably because your process of setting goals was not good enough.

Uncover the secrets of the successful goal setting and learn how to keep your momentum.

Visit here and get the bonus content (and more):

www.subscribepage.com/jeremycrownbonus

Chapter 1: Cognitive Behavior Therapy

Cognitive Behavioral Therapy (CBT) is a form of psychotherapeutic treatment that focuses on the feelings and thoughts that influence behavioral patterns in patients. CBT is an effective treatment for different disorders like addiction, anxiety, and phobias.

CBT is a short-term form of treatment and is advisable for patients who are struggling with a specific disorder. Through the treatment process, you learn how to identify thought patterns and how to take control and change them, especially those that have a negative impact on your emotions or behavior patterns. According to (Beck, Cognitive Behavior Therapy: Basics and Beyond, 2011), looking at your experience from this new perspective would probably make you feel better and lead to more functional behavior.

Understanding Cognitive Behavior Therapy

CBT borrows from the concept that your feelings and thoughts define your behavior. A good example is if you spend most of the time thinking about and worrying about air disasters, you will find it difficult to appreciate or even attempt air travel.

With CBT, you will learn that while it might not be possible to control the things that happen in your environment, or influence the stimuli around you, you have the power to control how you interpret them and, therefore, deal with them. Most of the time, patients struggle because they feel they are not in control of their feelings or thoughts.

Compared to most forms of therapy, CBT is affordable, and this is one reason it is increasingly becoming a preferable mode of treatment for mental health experts and other professionals.

Do You Need CBT?

Many people can find value in CBT today. You endure a stressful life each day at work. The corporate space is too stressful and balancing corporate needs and your personal life might not be easy. However, while CBT might be effective and useful to some people, this might not be the case for everyone.

You must conduct a needs assessment to determine whether CBT is what you need. Before you make up your mind, the following are some things you need to think about:

Are you comfortable thinking about what you feel? With CBT, you will be made aware of your emotions, anxieties, and things you have been avoiding. In the beginning, this can be distressing or uncomfortable, but as you work through it, you will open up more.

Do you need therapy? If you are dealing with complex problems, short-term therapy like CBT might not be useful. Depending on what you are dealing with, you might need therapy for a long time.

How much time can you spare? With CBT, you will be given exercises to perform after your sessions with the therapist. Therefore, you must commit some of your time toward completing these tasks. If you are unable to do so, CBT might not be ideal for you.

What Disorders Can CBT Treat?

CBT as a therapeutic process can treat conditions and disorders, including the following:

- Depression
- Conduct disorder
- Bipolar disorder
- ADHD
- Anxiety disorder
- Antisocial disorders (theft, lying, hurting animals, hurting other people)
- Substance abuse

- Awkward social skills
- Sleep disorders
- Schizophrenia
- Personality disorder
- Stress

How CBT Works

While other forms of psychoanalysis and therapy might need years of treatment, you only need around 20 sessions of CBT. Through these sessions, you will identify situations in your routine that are causing you problems. You define the thought patterns and distorted perceptions that might lead you down the wrong path.

As part of the treatment process, you might be asked to keep a journal where you will note down your reactions to events as they happen in your life. During your sessions with your therapist, you will talk about these reactions and how they make you feel.

Together with your therapist, you can address the negative thought patterns that manifest in your journal and change your perceptions with positive thoughts.

Choosing Your Therapist

You can perform CBT on your own without the help of a therapist. With the right self-help book or online guide, you can make tremendous progress. However, is it advisable?

According to relevant research, CBT is highly effective if you have a therapist working with you. Besides, you should attempt some therapy strategies only in the presence of a therapist, especially response prevention and systematic exposure.

Since your therapist is an important factor in your healing process, you should choose the one you are comfortable with. The relationship you have with the therapist will also determine how fast you respond to the changes you are making. Besides, discussing examples with the patient helps to illustrate that the patient's specific maladaptive cognitions are not unique, and are often experienced by many other people (Hofmann, 2011).

When in therapy, this is a non-judgmental space. Your therapist respects your reactions and views of situations and experiences you have gone through. They should inspire confidence and make you open up to them, which is how you make progress. A collaborative and conversational approach also makes you more active in the session and helps you feel better talking about things you would struggle to talk about with anyone else.

CBT Sessions

Therapists might have different approaches, but their sessions often have the same structure. For example, when you meet the therapist, you will talk about the reason you are seeing them. You will try to understand the problems you have and what you need to work on. At this juncture, you will also set the goals you need to achieve in these sessions. With that figured out, you can plan the sessions and the content together and discuss options that will help you deal with the problems mentioned.

As the session progresses, your therapist will recommend exercises, which are supposed to help you delve deeper into your thought process, behaviors, and feelings. You can use worksheets or diagrams to do this so you have a better understanding of what you are going through.

Expect assignments away from the therapy session. The therapist will recommend exercises you can perform at home or work when the session is over. These may or may not include people in your immediate surroundings. If so, make sure you choose people who are cooperative, understanding, and know what you are going through. Everyone around you should support you through this period.

When you come to the next session, you will go over the previous session. You will address the concerns you had earlier and the progress you have made since the last meeting. You will also address any concerns you have about the exercises you have been doing and what you think about the progress you are making so far.

Your therapist will also want to know how you feel about the whole experience. Remember that these sessions demand honesty, especially with yourself.

Types of Cognitive Behavior Therapy

The British Association of Behavioral and Cognitive Psychotherapies defines CBT as a range of therapies built on psychological principles and concepts of human behavior and emotion. These principles include different approaches for treating emotional disorders, including self-help and structured individual psychotherapy.

Different therapeutic approaches are involved in CBT. The following are most common in mental health:

Cognitive Therapy

This treatment helps you identify and change a distorted thought process or correct an inaccurate thought process, behavior, or emotional response.

Rational Emotive Behavior Therapy

This treatment is about identifying and changing irrational beliefs. Your therapist will help you challenge these beliefs, conquer them, and learn to notice them whenever they manifest and respond accordingly.

Dialectical Behavior Therapy

This therapy is about behaviors and thinking patterns. Strategies involved include mindfulness and emotional regulation.

Multimodal Therapy

This therapy deals with psychological issues from the perspective of connected modalities. These are the factors that might be responsible for the psychological trauma you might be experiencing. The seven modalities involved are biological or drug considerations, interpersonal factors, cognition, imagery, sensation, affect, and behavior.

Each of these therapy patterns is unique in their approach, but they all attempt to address thought patterns that might be responsible for the psychological distress you are going through. One of the pillars of CBT is to address an automatic negative thought process that manifests in the brain.

Automatic negative thought processes usually worsen the emotional concerns you are struggling with, such as anxiety and depression. These negative thoughts occur from time to time, and the more your brain accepts them as the new normal, the more likely they are to affect your mood.

Throughout the treatment process, your therapist will help you identify and examine these thoughts from an evidence-based approach. You try to find evidence that either refutes or supports these ideas. Such proof will help you find a more realistic and objective approach to addressing the factors that influence your moods.

By recognizing negativity in your environment, you can identify unrealistic thoughts and attempts to foster healthier relationships with people around you, fostering a healthier thought process.

Composition of Cognitive Behavior Therapy

The thoughts and feelings you experience help reinforce your beliefs, whether faulty or not. This is why troubled behavior eventually affects different aspects of your life, such as academics, family, work, and personal relationships. If you are struggling with confidence, for example, you will always feel inadequate and not worthy of the chances that come your way. You do not believe in your appearance or your ability to perform the task required, and because of this negative thought process, you avoid any situation that might warrant interaction with your peers or anyone who can challenge you. In the process, you start passing up chances for advancing your progress or career at work or in school.

Your therapist will help you identify the problematic beliefs keeping you from realizing your potential. The procedure is called functional analysis. At this juncture, you are both learning the impact that your situations, feelings, and thought process have on maladaptive behavior. Functional analysis might be difficult, especially if you have been dealing with introspection. However, if you work through it, functional analysis lays the perfect foundation for insight, reflection, and rediscovering yourself, which are essential in your healing process.

After functional analysis, your therapist will advance you to a behavioral approach. In this stage, they try to understand the behaviors that trigger the problem you are dealing with. You will also learn new skills applicable in real life, which will help you manage your situation better.

In a behavioral approach, consider someone battling drug addiction. You learn new skills to cope with your daily life and must rehearse these skills frequently. These skills come in handy if you find yourself in a situation that might encourage a relapse.

CBT is a step-by-step process toward positive behavioral change. You will learn how to handle yourself in a situation that might provoke the behavioral challenges you are facing. After this, you learn how to communicate with the people around you—your family, friends, workmates, and acquaintances. The people in your immediate environment play a significant role in your progress. They also help you achieve your therapy goals faster and help you feel less isolated.

Lessons from CBT

CBT is about imparting useful learning and coping skills, which will help you manage when faced with challenging situations. There are many ways of coping, and your therapist will help you figure out what works for you. One thing you will learn to overcome is avoidance.

You will learn pain management techniques. Pain is a normal part of life that we experience at different times and must work through. By avoiding your pain or situations you are uncomfortable with, you increase your fear. Through CBT, you will learn how to confront your worst fears. Confrontation is a manageable and gradual process, and in the end, you will have more faith in your ability to overcome your adversities.

CBT also teaches you how to explore your thoughts and desires. By writing things down, you have the chance to take a different perspective. You reflect on the notes you make, and this should help you learn how to change the negativity you have been feeling.

At the end of your CBT sessions, you should have also learned how to relate better to other people. If you make assumptions about them or their motivations, you will learn how to give them the benefit of the doubt, as you would expect them to do for you. Instead of always assuming the worst about people, you take a rational perspective of your interactions.

What if CBT Fails?

While CBT has proven to be successful for many people, not everyone gets as much help as they hope for. If at the end of your CBT sessions you see little or no progress, make this known to your therapist. You do not have to wait until the sessions are over.

CBT is about honesty, and you should be open about your perception of the sessions. Your therapist can also help you find ways to make the sessions better so you can get more out of them. If things do not work out, you can consider getting a different therapist. Even the most experienced cognitive therapists have difficulty with some patients (Beck, 2011).

If you do not strike a bond with your therapist, it might not be easy to open up. You will hold back on the things you feel are too dear to you. By shutting out your therapist, you will be placing stumbling blocks on your way to success.

Risks Associated with CBT

While there is minimal emotional risk linked to CBT, dealing with painful experiences and feelings is not easy, and this in itself can be a source of stress for you. Treatment in most cases means you must face circumstances you have been comfortable avoiding for a long time. However, you must understand that the goal of CBT is to help you learn to deal with the stress and anxiety that comes with facing your fears and dealing with them constructively and safely.

Chapter 2: Worry

Incapacitating phobia, panic attacks, unrelenting voices, obsessive thoughts—these keep you worried from time to time. You, however, do not need to succumb to this fear. You can get treatment for your worries. Exposure therapy and CBT have been particularly useful for patients in the past. These therapy sessions teach you how to manage your anxiety, stop worrying, and conquer your fears. By the end of your therapy sessions, you might realize that things were not as bad as you had earlier imagined.

According to research, therapy is one of the most effective options for dealing with worries. The reason is that unlike medical interventions, therapy addresses more than just the symptoms. It delves into the root of your problem. Through therapy, your therapist helps you understand why you are worried.

Therapy is also helpful because you will discover the real causes of your fears and worries. Everyone experiences fear and anxiety, and there's little doubt that some experiences would provoke fear in just about everyone (Clark & Beck, 2011). You will also learn how to ease into situations, relax, and get a different perspective. You can find alternative ways to handle the things you worry about, which are less frightening. You will learn how to cope and develop useful skills for problem-solving.

CBT is not just about giving you the tools you need to manage your worries. It is also about teaching you how to use the tools and skills you will learn.

The disorders that manifest through worry and anxiety might not be the same. Therefore, when you undergo therapy, your therapist will listen and address the symptoms unique to your diagnosis. Someone who has OCD, for example, will go through a different process compared to someone who is struggling with anxiety.

The duration of time you spend in therapy is also determined by the severity of your disorder. Most patients report significant progress within 8–10 sessions. It is, however, advisable to continue the sessions until your therapist advises you to stop.

Understanding Worry and Anxiety

You are probably feeling hopeless, vulnerable and unlovable right now. It is okay. This is a part of life. It might not feel like it right now, but worrying is more common than you know. You do not have to give in to your worries, however.

You can overcome that feeling of defeatism. You might feel you are unable to cope with something, or your input might not be appreciated, but all these are nothing but opinions and sentiments. They are not true.

You might even feel afraid and scared, but do not shut down just yet. Do not isolate yourself or avoid facing the things you are worried about.

CBT for Worry and Anxiety

CBT is one of the most preferred therapies for anxiety disorders. It has been used effectively for persons with a phobia, generalized anxiety disorder, panic disorder, and many other conditions. CBT helps you learn about the negative thoughts that inhibit your progress. This comes from understanding how you look at yourself in your immediate environment.

There are two elements of CBT that help in treating your anxieties. Cognitive therapy addresses the way your thoughts make you anxious. Behavior therapy, on the other hand, studies the way you react or behave in circumstances that might invoke anxiety.

Your thoughts determine your worries. Most people think external events or situations determine how they feel about something, but this is not true. Your perception of a given situation will eventually determine what you feel about it and how you respond to it.

Challenging Your Thought Process

When dealing with anxiety, your therapist will help you learn more about your thoughts and change them (cognitive restructuring). There are negative thoughts you might experience which increase your feeling of anxiety. The goal of CBT is to help you do away with these thoughts and instead replace them with positive and realistic thoughts. The procedure then takes the following steps:

Identify the Negative Thoughts

When you are suffering from an anxiety disorder, you tend to believe situations are more dangerous than they are. Let's take the example of someone who has a phobia of germs. Shaking another person's hand will continuously have them worried that they might catch something. In fact, to them, this might even be life-threatening.

An average person will see this as irrational, taking the fear out of hand. However, if you have an anxiety disorder, rational thought is not a luxury you can afford. Your therapist will help you identify these irrational thoughts.

Challenge Negative Thoughts

Having identified the anxiety-provoking thoughts, you need to challenge them. You need to question why you are thinking about these things. Do you have a reason to believe your fears will come true? What is the worst that could happen? What if, instead of running away from your fear, you face it?

You will weigh the pros and cons of your actions or responses to anxiety-provoking situations. Avoiding your fears will only make you create more fears to run away from. When you are afraid of dealing with something, you will soon fear dealing with anything else closely related to it. This is how fear manifests.

Replace Negative Thoughts

Once you realize nothing can happen to you if you stop worrying, the next step is to change the negative thoughts. Replace them with something more real. You can challenge cognitive distortions that make you anxious by creating new thoughts which are positive, more accurate, and realistic.

One way of doing this is to write some calming sentences that you can tell yourself whenever you face any adversity. Such statements help you anticipate anxious moments, and instead of sending you into panic mode, they will calm you down.

Your therapist may also help you come up with realistic, calming statements you can say to yourself when you're facing or anticipating a situation that generally sends your anxiety levels soaring.

Negative thoughts embed themselves into your brain because most of these develop over a long time. For most people, this happens throughout their life. You will have to practice a lot to break these bad habits, which is why you will receive assignments to perform once the session with your therapist is up for the day. When dealing with anxiety, your therapist might also ask you to note down when you feel anxious and how you feel physically and mentally when that happens.

Exposure Therapy for Anxiety

There is nothing pleasant about anxiety. By default, people tend to avoid things that make them anxious. Other than creating inconveniences in your life, avoiding confrontation with these situations only prolongs an unavoidable experience. At some point in life, you will have to overcome your fears. Why prolong it when you can do it right now?

Besides, by prolonging the confrontations you are supposed to have right now, you are holding yourself back, preventing yourself from experiencing the beauty of life. Do not hold back from exploiting the opportunities that come your way. Sadly, this only increases your anxiety.

In exposure therapy, your therapist will expose you to the things that make you anxious. The idea here is to get you used to them, to make you realize that what you were afraid of cannot harm you. Your therapist can either get you to confront your fears in real life or in an imaginary setting.

Systematic Desensitization

Systematic desensitization is a part of exposure therapy used in CBT. If you cannot face your worst nightmare right away, you can start working with something smaller and work your way up. It is a gradual approach that helps you improve your confidence, learn skills that will be useful in controlling your panic, and challenge your worst fears.

There are three elements of systematic desensitization:

- Relaxation skills
- Step-by-step list
- Working through the steps

Relaxation Skills

You will learn a relaxation technique from your therapist, and there are many you can choose from. You can start with progressive deep breathing or muscle relaxation. You can practice these techniques in your session, or you can also do them at home.

The relaxation skills you learn are useful when you get anxious. When you are anxious, you may hyperventilate or tremble, or exhibit other symptoms. These skills will help you calm down and look at things clearly.

Step-by-Step List

You already know the final goal you are working toward. From here, you will create a list of things you need to accomplish before you get to the ultimate goal. As you write these down, you must be specific and make sure the objectives are realistic.

Working through the Steps

Your therapist will guide you as you work on your list one item at a time. The idea here is to make sure you address each circumstance until you manage your fears. It might not be immediate, but after a while, you will learn to conquer your fears.

While working through these steps, you will still need to remember the relaxation techniques you learned earlier. If things are getting too intense, you can take a step back and relax. After that, go back to the situation and proceed until you can conquer your fears.

Managing Anxiety through CBT

You must be committed to overcoming anxiety. There is no quick fix for it. It might take a long time, but your dedication will make a big difference. You might even feel worse before things change for the better. Follow the guidelines of your therapist, and you should be fine. When the anxious mind takes over, the automatic response is to escape or avoid the source of the anxiety (Clark & Beck, 2011).

Even while you are undergoing therapy, you can make some changes in your life to support this recovery process. Positivity is one such change you need in your life. Everything in your social life plays a role in anxiety. Therefore, you should find ways of promoting positive vibes, vitality, relaxation, and a positive outlook on life.

How much do you know about anxiety? Understanding what you are dealing with is one of the first steps toward quick recovery. Read more on anxiety. Learning might not help you find a cure, but it will help you understand why you are going through the things you are. Learning will also help you appreciate progress and notice the gradual impact you are making in life.

Talk to people. You have a better chance of healing faster when you are interacting with people who are positive about your progress. Establish good relations and connections with people. Talk to your family members and friends. Isolation leads to loneliness, and this lays the foundation for anxiety. Reach out to people often to weed out the risk of vulnerability.

Change your lifestyle if you can. You should practice healthy habits like eating a balanced diet, exercising often, and drinking a lot of water. Drugs and alcohol will never help you manage anxiety. They can make you pretend your problems are gone, but when the high dies down, anxiety will still be there. Avoid nicotine and caffeine because they worsen your situation.

CBT Toolbox

There are a lot of things that can make you worry. Spare a few minutes and identify them using this guide, answering simple questions to get an insight into the struggle you are going through.

Identifying Worry Triggers

I worry a lot when:

1.

2.

3.

4.

I have felt like this before. When was it?

1.

2.

3.

4.

Certain things always happen in my life before I get this feeling. List them.

1.

2.

3.

4.

Worry, anxiety and stress have the same feelings, but they might manifest differently. When I am worried, these are some of the things I feel I am going through:

1.

2.

3.

4.

Identify Distorted Thoughts

We need to figure out the things you think about when worried, and find a way to change that into positive thoughts. Whenever I feel this way, I do the following:

1.

2.

3.

4.

To avoid feeling this worried, these are my go-to escapes:

1.

2.

3.

4.

Some of the things I avoid doing when I am this worried include:

1.

2.

3.

4.

There might always be a consequence of an action. When you are worried, you might fail to do something you should have. Let's identify some of the consequences. Think about the last time you felt this way, and list some of the consequences you faced after that:

1.

2.

3.

4.

Alternative Coping Skills

Since we have identified what might have gone wrong, let's try and learn a few new tricks that will make a difference.

Whenever I get this feeling, the following are some things I will try to do to improve my predicament:

1.

2.

3.

4.

Challenge the Distorted Thoughts

The thing about distorted thoughts is that you tend to rationalize without proof. This is what keeps you worried. We will try to use an evidence-based approach to address your concerns. Think about some of the things you automatically assumed would go wrong, and then write a logical response to it, something that would be evidence based.

I will give you two examples to get you going:

Distortion: She will turn me down if I ask her out.

Logic: Until I ask her out, I will never know. Maybe she's just as nervous about this as I am. I am asking her out. What's there to lose?

Distortion: I will not attend that class. It is too difficult for me.

Logic: What if I give it a try? There are other students in that class, right? They too might be struggling as I am. Besides, I can always ask the teacher to explain something I don't understand, after class.

1. Distortion:

Logic:

2. Distortion:

Logic:

3. Distortion:

Logic:

4. Distortion:

Logic:

CHAPTER 3:
SHYNESS AND SOCIAL ANXIETY

Social phobia (social anxiety disorder) refers to a feeling of nervousness or tension when you are in a situation that involves meeting other people. Some people are good at hiding it, or they find a way to keep themselves occupied throughout such interactions.

It causes distress that can advance to agoraphobia or depression. These are psychological disorders that are increasingly claiming the lives of people at a young age.

For social anxiety, CBT is one of the best treatments. You learn how to react to feelings and thoughts; you learn how to engage in situations or circumstances that make you afraid. Through CBT, you will also learn to identify places where you have a deficit in social skills and practice how to make up for the deficit.

Shyness

Do you feel uncomfortable when you have attention? You might not know you do, but if you get nervous or blush, you might need to consider CBT. This form of shyness is common in many people. When you are shy, you will try to find ways of coping with the situation or avoiding it altogether. To protect yourself, you can learn new avoidance behavior. Shyness is a form of social anxiety.

Did you know social anxiety is one of the most common emotional health disorders? It comes third after addiction and depression. Shyness can be debilitating. You might have seen people who are very comfortable in their shyness, but there are others who struggle.

Shyness makes you worry all the time about what people are thinking about you. You fear they will see you, that they will notice how you walk, or some other flaw you might have. When you feel this uncomfortable around people, you cannot relax around them or interact with them freely.

The life of a shy person is full of fear and worry. You keep perceiving situations to be dangerous. Instead of looking forward to interacting with people, you are afraid of them. You worry about the reactions people have and the possibility of negative bias toward you.

Through CBT, you will learn useful skills that can help you deal with the problem at hand by changing the way you feel about and around people. Stand up to your fears and assume a rational approach to interactions you were once afraid of.

Through CBT, you will learn that your idea of mental processing and filtering events around you is not right. Once you accept this, you can then work on a way to change that. You will use an evidence-based approach to rationalize your experiences.

Understanding Social Anxiety

Social anxiety is the fear of embarrassment or judgment by others. It is an extreme concern that can interfere with your normal routine. This disorder can make you afraid of going to work or school, locking yourself in the house because you fear what people will think about you.

Like many other anxiety conditions, social anxiety operates as a vicious cycle. You anticipate social encounters with some degree of trepidation, then you find yourself in the social situation experiencing unhelpful thoughts and actions that drive up your anxiety, and then afterward you rehash and brood over the social encounter, which only exaggerates the dread with which you anticipate the next social interaction (Clark & Beck, 2011).

You will feel self-conscious and embarrassed. Understand that at some point in life, everyone has undergone social anxiety. Whenever you are meeting people for the first time, you will worry about that meeting. What if they do not like you? What if you do not like the experience? How should you behave around them?

These are common thoughts that happen in interactive spaces all the time. Public speakers struggle with this a lot. However, the difference here is that these feelings manifest just before you get out of your comfort zone and interact with other people. On the other hand, a person struggling with social anxiety disorder might get worried about their fears days or weeks before they have to face these situations.

Social anxiety can make you afraid of doing things with people, or in front of them. There are different triggers for this kind of anxiety. Even though many people know their fears are unrealistic, they still struggle to stay in control. As a result, they shy away from anything they feel might be humiliating. For some people, this might mean avoiding a select few situations, while others might do away with all social interaction altogether.

What Causes Social Anxiety?

Different factors might be responsible for social anxiety. For some people, it can run in the family. The following are three important factors that might be responsible for your case of social anxiety disorder:

Family Environment

You learn so many things from your family as you grow up. You will pick up attitudes about yourself from the way your family relates with you. These can be inherited over generations as you keep interacting with different members of the extended family.

Children who grow up around parents who have social anxiety disorder might struggle to interact with people around them, even if they do not have social anxiety themselves. If you grew up in a critical environment as a child, you will rarely see yourself any better and will get so used to criticism that you expect it.

However, it is also essential to address the fact that this environment does not necessarily have to map the course of your life. You can free yourself from such anxiety if you take the right steps, including seeing a CBT therapist.

Genetics

Scientific evidence suggests that genetics can also determine whether you develop social anxiety disorder. Therefore, this can be passed down from parent to child. It can even occur as a result of the environment where the child lives, as highlighted in the familial discourse above.

Experiences

You might have grown up a normal child, free of genetic difficulties, social anxiety, or familial influence. However, you may still develop social anxiety disorder through your life experiences. If you have a speech impairment or any notable physical defect at birth, you might develop social anxiety because you worry about what people say or think about you. Bullying at school or any other social institution can also induce social anxiety because you worry about criticism from those around you or always expect harsh judgment.

Diagnosing Social Anxiety

Most cases of social anxiety are evident in your youth. If left untreated, social anxiety can haunt you for a long time. It is also possible to experience social anxiety over a specific situation but generalize in some others. This explains why you might feel anxious around strangers in a congregation, but comfortable around people you know.

A therapist will discuss the challenges you are going through and accurately diagnose social anxiety. Fear is one thing your therapist will be on the lookout for. They will be looking for fear as a response to one or more circumstances. Fear often comes about because you are afraid of scrutiny in a prolonged conversation when dating, meeting new people, or eating with strangers.

You worry that you might do something that would make you stand out negatively or something that would make people judge you. You are also afraid of saying the wrong thing, so you keep quiet to avoid embarrassment.

CBT Toolbox

The following are some simple exercises that will help you learn more about your social anxiety and how to deal with it.

Identifying Anxiety Triggers

I feel uncomfortable and socially anxious in these situations:

1.

2.

3.

4.

The last time I felt this way was when

1.

2.

3.

4.

Identify Distorted Thoughts

Whenever I am feeling shy, these are some of the things that go through my mind

1.

2.

3.

4.

Each time I feel cornered and shy, I feel the need to engage fight or flight, and do the following to escape the attention.

1.

2.

3.

4.

When I feel shy, these are some of the things that I cannot do:

1.

2.

3.

4.

List down some of the opportunities that have passed you by, by virtue of the fact that you were too shy to exploit them.

1.

2.

3.

4.

Alternative Coping Skills

I do not want to struggle with shyness all my life. These are some of the things I will try to do whenever I get that feeling:

1.

2.

3.

4.

Challenge the Distorted Thoughts

What's the worst that could possibly happen if you conquered your fears and stood up for what you believe in? The distortion is the worst-case scenario – what you think might happen. The logic is what is real – that which happens when you address your fears.

1. Distortion:

Logic:

2. Distortion:

Logic:

3. Distortion:

Logic:

4. Distortion:

Logic:

Chapter 4:
Negative Self-Talk

Talking to yourself is not something new or weird. Everyone talks to themselves from time to time. You might hold discussions about things you can change and some about things you cannot change. Self-talk is a term often used to describe the dialogues we have in our minds, or "what we tell ourselves" (Riggenbach, 2013).

Self-talk is a habit you form to respond to different experiences. It is also an internal critic that can either prop you up or bring you down. It all depends on the voice you choose to listen to. If you are constantly negative and pessimistic about life, you will do more harm than good. For example, you might constantly remind yourself of how bad you are and that you cannot become any better.

This defeatist voice manifests, and you start blaming yourself even for things beyond your control. The problem with negative self-talk is that you end up setting high standards or unrealistic expectations; they only make you hopeless and increase your anxiety. Hopelessness and fear are not constructive. Instead, they suppress your positivity.

Understanding Negative Self-Talk

Cognitive therapy builds on the concept that what you feel is a direct result of the way you think. If you always think of negative things, these eventually manifest into negative moods. Through CBT, however, you can learn how to improve your thought process. With the help of your therapist, you will learn how to identify unrealistic thought patterns and change them for the better. These unrealistic thought patterns are cognitive distortions.

There are three common cognitive distortions that most people struggle with as they go about their daily schedules:

Should Syndrome

The "should syndrome" is about creating strict rules about how you should act around people. It also applies to how you expect people to behave around you. You feel guilty when you break any of these rules. This syndrome also comes with regret. A good example is when something happens and you tell yourself, "*I should have prepared well for this.*"

Instead of wallowing in regret, you need to think of how to realign your expectations so that they are in line with your abilities. It is okay to challenge yourself to do better, but at the same time, you also should keep realistic goals. You might not achieve everything you set out to do, but try to do so. Always try to recognize and appreciate your efforts.

Catastrophizing

Catastrophizing happens when you jump to conclusions or generalize because of an isolated incident. In most cases, you catastrophize without proper evidence. Let's say you are trying to lose weight and in the first few days of exercising, you gain weight instead. You might generalize and say exercise is not working and switch to a fad diet instead.

To overcome this negativity, you must take time to address the unique challenges you are going through. There is a good reason you are gaining weight instead of losing it. Has something changed in your immediate environment? Is there something you started eating? Are you on medication? Is it merely muscle weight?

Some exercise routines don't take effect immediately. It will take a while before you start seeing results. Your body might also be responding to the new stressful situation you put yourself through when working out, and after a while, you will notice the results. Instead of catastrophizing, try to analyze why things are happening the way they are.

Mind Reading

Mind reading is about drawing conclusions. When you are talking to or interacting with someone, you assume you already know what they are feeling or what they are thinking. Say you have been communicating with someone for a long time and, for some reason, they have not been in contact with you. It is easy to conclude that they do not care or think about you anymore, yet this is not true.

There are many reasons someone might not be in touch with you. They might be busy. If you give it some time, they might get in touch with you once they clear their schedule. Alternatively, you can try reaching out to them to find out how they are doing.

One of the best ways of overcoming mind reading is to be proactive. Instead of waiting for someone to contact you, call them. Perhaps they are out of town and could not get proper network access. Maybe they have had a horrible day and are just exhausted.

These three are the common cognitive distortions that you might struggle through each day. It is easy to see how they can evolve into negative self-talk and affect your life severely. If you cannot deal with these, it is time you consider cognitive therapy.

CBT Procedure for Negative Self-Talk

As you work through your challenges with your therapist, you learn to identify the cognitive distortions whenever they occur, refute them, and replace them with realistic, rational thoughts. One problem with cognitive distortions is that they tend to push you toward feeling helpless and hopeless. If you replace these distortions, you will have a better, productive, and optimistic outlook on life.

When dealing with cognitive distortions, CBT outlines a three-step process, as follows:

Step 1: Identifying Cognitive Distortions

You must first recognize an iterative thought process before you can change it. Identifying cognitive distortions might not be easy, given that you might have done this so many times that the thoughts manifest as automatic responses whenever you find yourself in a given situation.

In most cases, the thoughts can ingrain in your mind to the point where they become institutionalized. When you speak to a therapist, they can help you identify these thoughts. Write them down if possible to help create some distance between your thoughts and yourself.

Most of these thoughts manifest because you take them for granted. Since they are autonomous, you might not recognize them immediately. This step demands patience as you try to learn more about yourself.

Step 2: Evaluating Your Thought Process

Having identified the thoughts and written them down, you should evaluate them and find out how irrational they are. How do you determine whether the feelings are irrational? Look at each thought you wrote down and ask yourself what evidence you have to support your thought process. You will soon realize that you barely have proof to back any of the irrational thoughts that have been making it difficult for you to make progress in life.

Step 3: Replacing Unrealistic Thoughts

This is the last step, and it is about making changes. Work with your therapist to identify and propose a better understanding of the experiences you go through. You can find an alternative way of interpreting your thoughts or take an evidence-based approach to evaluate the same.

In the example we used earlier about losing weight, you can assure yourself that even though you have relapsed, you have also noted progress since you started working out. This sentiment should give you hope. Instead of giving up altogether, you can talk to someone—a trainer, perhaps—about how they can help you turn things around.

Positivity vs. Realism

As you go through CBT to change negative self-talk, your emphasis should be on realistic thoughts. While it is okay to think positively, you should focus on practical thoughts. If you do not address them carefully, positive thoughts can cause you to set insane standards you might not be able to meet.

What you think or say to yourself about everyday situations in your life will strongly influence how you feel and what you do. Negative self-talk can cause unpleasant emotions and self-defeating behaviors (Gregory, 2010).

CBT should help you understand your current predicament. You must realize and accept the negative things happening in your life and address them in a realistic and balanced way. You will be retraining yourself, learning new habits that eventually help you move in the right direction. Progress in CBT is gradual and might take time. However, the benefits when you complete the therapy sessions can change your life.

CBT Toolbox

You might not intentionally encourage yourself into negative self-talk, but it happens anyway. Let's try and work through it with this simple exercise.

Identifying Negativity Triggers

I tend to patronize myself a lot when:

1.

2.

3.

4.

I discourage myself from time to time. The last time this happened was:

1.

2.

3.

4.

List a few things that happen around you, which make you doubt your ability to do something.

1.

2.

3.

4.

Identify Distorted Thoughts

Soon after I discourage myself from doing something, I do the following:

1.

2.

3.

4.

To avoid the negativity, these are my go-to escapes:

1.

2.

3.

4.

Some of the things that I have always avoided because I feel I am not good enough include:

1.

2.

3.

4.

Out of negative self-talk, I have had to sit back and watch others shine. These are some of the accolades I have missed out on:

1.

2.

3.

4.

Alternative Coping Skills

I want to live a positive life. Instead of this negativity, I will try the following to help me believe in myself:

1.

2.

3.

4.

Challenge the Distorted Thoughts

This is about conquering your fears. The negativity makes you afraid to unleash your potential. There is no evidence to support the negative thought. However, let's try and reason out your thoughts with some positivity.

I will give you an example to get you going:

Distortion: I cannot be the team captain.

Logic: Well, the coach is recommending me for a reason. There's something they have seen in me that I might not have noticed yet. Perhaps I should talk to them and find out more about their decision.

1. Distortion:

Logic:

2. Distortion:

Logic:

3. Distortion:

Logic:

4. Distortion:

Logic:

Chapter 5:
Low Self-Esteem

Self-esteem is your perception of yourself. It is how you believe other people see you when they interact with you. It refers to the beliefs and thoughts you have about yourself, your future, your world, and everything else about you.

If you have a low perception of yourself, you will probably be overwhelmed and feel low. You will struggle to interact with your peers or fit in because you always feel you are sticking out like a sore thumb. Healthy esteem does not mean thinking you are the best at everything – it means being comfortable with yourself even when you are not. It is accepting yourself, with all your strengths and weaknesses, while still taking opportunities for self-development (Wilding & Palmer, 2017).

When you start thinking in this way, it is not a fleeting negative thought, but low self-esteem manifests depending on the situation or circumstances. These feelings happen from time to time, and after a while, your brain gets used to them.

If you have low self-esteem, getting into a difficult predicament will activate the negative beliefs. You feel everything will go wrong, and this automatically ends up creating negative moods and a feeling of anxiety.

To deal with this, most people try to avoid meeting friends or going out. Even simple things like grocery shopping will be difficult for you because you are afraid of what people will think about you when they see you. You are so scared of being criticized or judged that you start isolating yourself, and before long, you get used to isolation.

When you are in an unavoidable situation where you have to interact with people, you find yourself trying to please them. You go out of your way to make sure they are happy around you. You are afraid of being abandoned, unloved, or rejected, so you conform, even if it goes against everything you believe in.

Understanding Low Self-Esteem

The problem with having low self-esteem is that it eats into your confidence. What you are feeling right now might be taking a toll on you. You probably feel undeserving and vulnerable, like people can see or find you at your worst. However, this is not true. These are concerns that have been created in your mind, and they are not true.

You are not weak or a loser. You are stronger than you think you are. The mental filters you have created can be overcome. Do not let one bad experience determine the rest of your future. Just because you have failed once, doesn't mean you will fail all the time. Pick yourself up from this and you will be better than you could ever have imagined.

Using CBT for Low Self-Esteem

One approach that CBT uses to help you overcome esteem issues is to look at the core beliefs you are struggling with as mere opinions, which they are. There is no factual representation to what you believe. There is no evidence that people dislike you. It might surprise you that people like you more than you know.

These beliefs keep manifesting in your brain through negative behavior and thoughts. The more you think about them, the more your brain accepts them as the new normal. Strategies are in place that you can use to combat this. Together with your therapist, you can work on developing a set of new behavior patterns.

The idea here is to show you the lack of evidence to support the negative beliefs you have about yourself. It is to show you a logical representation of things as they are and not as you think they are. CBT, therefore, targets the erroneous thought patterns. It is about retraining your brain to see things in a more functional and balanced way.

If someone is not giving you attention, you might think they are ignoring you because they do not appreciate you the way you need them to. You might even think you are not good enough to warrant their attention. However, this is far from the truth. They could simply be preoccupied with other things. They might be struggling with something you do not know about.

Instead of assuming that things are so bad, you can make a move, call them, and talk to them. It might even surprise you to learn that they were having a dreadful day and your call made things better for them. Reaching out will improve your mood and make you feel good about yourself. With CBT, you try to retrain the brain to disapprove the initial negative thoughts you have about your perception of yourself and see things differently.

Building Self-Esteem

Self-esteem is an aggregate of all the thoughts you have when thinking about your confidence in your ability. If you have good self-esteem, you are more confident in yourself than someone who doesn't. Low self-esteem happens especially when you are prone to self-criticism. On many occasions, low self-esteem can cause depression or anxiety.

CBT is one of the best treatment options for many psychological concerns. It is a brief form of treatment that addresses the core problems you are dealing with. While most treatment methods will discuss relationships and your early developmental history, CBT addresses the things you are struggling with at this moment.

CBT treatment for low self-esteem might include any of the following processes:

- Mindfulness training
- Roleplay
- Assertiveness training
- Learning social skills
- Behavioral experiments and activation
- Study of the current schema
- Cognitive restructuring

Cognitive Restructuring

In cognitive restructuring, your therapist will try to identify negative thought patterns and replace them with positive ones. For self-esteem, this involves identifying the negative things you think about yourself and your abilities. It is about finding out the distortions in your thought process.

There are many times when you feel you are a failure in life, perhaps because you have a deficit in some skills, or because you had a bad day. These things should not get you down. Negative self-talk will only make matters worse. Everyone has a bad day from time to time, so this should not go to your head.

Behavioral Activation

If you have low self-esteem, you avoid places or situations you are uncomfortable with. Anything you feel you might not excel in will automatically move lower in your list of priorities. The problem with this is that you keep having fewer opportunities to engage in rewarding experiences. Such tendencies soon spiral into depression.

Behavioral activation is a process within which your therapist will help you change this cycle. You have a disconnect in certain social circles, and your therapist will help you re-engage, reconnect, and enjoy some of the most rewarding experiences you have been missing out on.

Assertiveness Training

If you have low self-esteem, you are afraid of people. You are scared to ask for something you want and also struggle to turn down requests or tell someone what you feel. This lack of assertiveness is dangerous, especially in a social construct.

People will find it easy to get away with anything at your expense. Others will use you as a stepping stone to their success. Through assertiveness training, you will learn new skills to help you speak with authority about what you feel or what you want without worrying about the damage this might do to your relationships.

Most of the time, you worry about sacrificing your relationship if you are assertive, but this is never the case. It is this unfounded fear that your therapist will tackle in assertiveness training.

Problem-Solving Approach

You feel helpless in many situations if you have low self-esteem. Whenever you have a problem, you do not think you have the strength or mentality to deal with it. You worry about failing if you try to solve it. You worry about what people will think about your attempt.

Through problem-solving training, your therapist will help you identify ways of solving problems. You will learn how to identify ideal solutions, especially using the resources you have at your disposal. You will learn how to be courageous enough to put a plan in motion and solve the problem.

Social Skills Training

Low self-esteem and social skill deficit go hand in hand. You struggle to interact with people. You find it difficult to fit into any social circle, even with people you should consider your peers, people you share so much in common with.

Social skills training is crucial, as it will help you learn to improve your interactions with the people around you. You will learn to reward social behavior, a positive approach to interactions, and how to be comfortable around people.

Low self-esteem centers on your perception of yourself. CBT helps you understand the cause of these cognitive perceptions. When you understand how you create meaning from the situations you are in, it is easier to reframe your thought process and improve your esteem. Your therapist will listen and help you refocus different aspects of your life to improve your behavior patterns.

CBT Toolbox

While most people consider themselves to have low self-esteem, it can be worse in others, and it is even bad when you do not know when it happens.

Identifying Low Self-Esteem Triggers

I struggle with low self-esteem when:

1.

2.

3.

4.

These are the times when I have the lowest opinion of myself:

1.

2.

3.

4.

Here is a list of things that have happened in my life that make me think so low of myself.

1.

2.

3.

4.

Identify Distorted Feelings

How do I feel when I have a low opinion of myself?

1.

2.

3.

4.

To avoid dealing with my esteem issues, these are some of the things I prefer:

1.

2.

3.

4.

Some of the things that I have always avoided because I feel I am not good enough include:

1.

2.

3.

4.

List down some of the consequences you have endured as a result of low self-esteem:

1.

2.

3.

4.

Alternative Coping Skills

I want to live a positive life. Instead of this negativity, I will try the following to help me believe in myself the next time I think so poorly of myself:

1.

2.

3.

4.

Challenge the Distorted Thoughts

This is about conquering your fears. The negativity makes you afraid to unleash your potential. However, you are not as bad as you feel you are.

I will give you an example to get you going:

Distortion: My project failed. I am the worst and do not deserve another project

Logic: This is just one failed attempt. No one has 100% good days. Besides, I have performed well in other projects before, so this was an isolated case. I believe I can learn from this and perform better on the next project.

1. *Distortion:*

Logic:

2. *Distortion:*

Logic:

3. *Distortion:*

Logic:

4. *Distortion:*

Logic:

Chapter 6:
Low Confidence

Low confidence is one of the underlying reasons behind depression and anxiety. Since you do not have faith in your ability, you cannot take risks. You handle tasks assigned to you half-heartedly because you cannot find the energy or courage to give anything your best shot. You have convinced yourself for a long time that you do not have the guts to do anything correctly.

These thought patterns eventually end up affecting your performance. Over time, your brain enforces this lack of confidence in your ability, and it becomes a vicious cycle you can barely get out of.

In CBT, your therapist uses a combination of methods to change your dysfunctional thought process. They try to do away with the negative thought patterns that have kept you stuck and hold you back from realizing your potential.

Negative, ineffective behavior and self-defeatist thoughts are just some things that end up causing low confidence. Your therapist will try to teach you how to behave and think like someone who has a strong belief in their ability, someone confident about their contribution to their environment.

Understanding Low Confidence

Things might not be going your way right now, but that does not mean it is the end. This is not the end. You still have a chance to make a difference. When things are not going your way, it is easy to feel you are not putting in enough effort. You might even feel you are not good enough.

Nothing should stand in your way. That feeling of defection you are feeling right now is just a smokescreen. Believe in yourself. Believe in your ability to challenge and conquer your fears. It is amazing how much you can achieve if you just believe in yourself. Do not give up just yet.

CBT Interventions for Low Confidence

Cognitive Restructuring

Cognitive restructuring is an intervention where your therapist identifies your negative thought process. They focus on the negative assumptions you have made about yourself and help you find a better way of tackling difficult situations.

For someone low on confidence, cognitive restructuring is mainly about dealing with the assumptions you have made about your inability to perform, your failure to accomplish tasks, and the harsh judgments you keep passing on yourself. It is about helping you find a positive, useful, and realistic way of thinking about situations you engage in each day.

Systematic Exposure

Systematic exposure is about facing your demons. If you have low confidence, it is easy to run away from certain situations you are worried about. The concept of systematic exposure builds on the pretext that by avoiding situations that fill you with fear, you are holding yourself back from evaluating your abilities.

If you do not try, you might never know how you would have performed. Perhaps you are not as bad as you think you are. Perhaps you are the best person for the job. But since you are afraid to try and you keep running away from it, you will never know for sure.

Through systematic exposure, your therapist encourages you to open up and face the situations you continuously avoid. By dealing with these situations, you will realize that you are not as bad as you had otherwise imagined.

You realize that things are not as difficult as you thought they were, and this makes you more confident. It helps you overcome anxiety in such situations. For low confidence, systematic exposure involves working with your therapist to plan activities you would typically avoid. After planning, you must frequently power through these activities.

Your therapist might ask you to try speaking up in meetings or debating. The more you practice these activities, the easier it will be for you to master the courage to be bolder in your interactions.

Mindfulness Training

Mindfulness is a skill that helps you focus on your present. Often, you find your mind wandering, thinking about things you cannot influence, worrying, or deep in thought. The problem with this is that you fight yourself often. You give yourself a difficult time as you keep second-guessing yourself.

Through mindfulness training, you will learn to give yourself a breather. In a difficult situation, you focus on how to improve your confidence. Even if you fail at what you are doing, you should not let it get you down. Dust yourself off and move on.

Mindfulness training also goes hand in hand with solution finding. If you are low on confidence, you will continuously see yourself as a victim. There are many situations you find yourself in which you can get out of. However, since you are not confident in your ability to find solutions to your problems, you wallow in pain and grief. An unhealthy status quo should not manifest longer than necessary. Believe in yourself and in your ability to find a solution.

CBT Exercises for Low Confidence

Feeling good about yourself and your ability demands internal effort. Your therapist will help you find realistic ways to deal with the things you worry about, the ones that are holding you back. Together, you will identify the patterns that exist in your brain about your confidence and try to change them and use the new patterns you learn to improve your confidence.

Exercise 1: Perspective

At times, you feel you are only as good as other people say you are. This is not true. The truth is that you should define your strength based on your criteria and not a vague reality that has been forced onto you by someone else. You know your strengths and weaknesses.

There is nothing wrong with reflecting or comparing yourself with someone as long as you do not take it too far. Comparisons should help you challenge yourself to do better and improve yourself, not cause you to doubt your abilities.

There are situations in your environment that might make it difficult to thrive, hurting your confidence. These are the moments you should discuss with your therapist and find a way of conquering them.

Note down a few aspects of your day that are challenging. Write down the positive things you have done that day, things you conquered, and how it made you feel. Look at the list, and the sentiments attached and list them in order of those that made you feel most important and appreciated.

You will notice that the things which concern your personality rank highest. This might seem obvious, but it means that confidence is all about perspective and perceptions. This acts as a reminder that the core of your self-confidence depends more on the effort you make personally than on what others think about you. The accomplishments you made, especially with challenging tasks, are all dependent on your ability. It is your self-belief that keeps getting you through.

Exercise 2: Criticism

You are your own worst enemy. Few people find as many faults with you as you do. You criticize yourself often. Even when you work hard, you still feel you did not do your best. You can change the way you talk to yourself. Instead of the negative thoughts, you can change the narrative and replace it with positive and realistic dialogue.

Encourage yourself to go the extra mile. Appreciate the effort you are making and believe that tomorrow will be a better day. You might not always have a good day, but giving up should never be an option.

Stand in front of a mirror and talk to yourself. Listen to the words that come to mind. How critical are you? Reflect upon those words. Do they remind you of someone in particular? Do they remind you of something you have heard for a long time?

While reflecting on those words, ask yourself how valid they are. Do you believe they are an accurate representation of your current predicament? Rethink those narratives and imagine you were saying them to your friend, younger siblings, or even your child. What tone would you use? Now look into the mirror again and use the exact tone you would use, but this time, speak to yourself. You would probably try to use a reassuring voice when advising someone. Why then, do you criticize yourself? Treat yourself with the same care you would offer someone else.

When you practice internal dialogue and make it consistent and supportive, it is easy to change the way you see yourself. Instead of trying to fix yourself because of your constant criticism, you can make peace with the person you are. Work with what you have.

When you wake up in the morning, assure yourself you will be the best version of yourself that day. In your internal dialogue, be kind to yourself. Life is already hard enough—why make things harder?

Exercise 3: Perfection

It is easy to confuse organization with perfection. You come across people who seem to get things right all the time. Through your interactions with these individuals, you feel they are perfect. Perfection is a fallacy that consumes most people, and you should not worry about it.

You focus a lot on the good things that someone else does, the success they achieve, without looking at their journey to get there. We are a result-oriented generation. Everyone seems to be excited about the destination but ignore the journey.

No one is perfect. The sooner you get that into your head, the sooner you will start appreciating yourself for who you are. This will also help you improve your confidence. You need to believe in your ability, especially if you did your best. You must also acknowledge that you might be unable to show up with the same level of enthusiasm and energy tomorrow as you did yesterday.

People have bad days they barely talk about. Those in their immediate circles may or may not know about that. The same applies to you. Do not focus so much on the result that you lose track of the process.

Processes can be daunting. Some processes drain all the energy out of you; some even drain the life out of you. However, believe in yourself. This is the only thing that matters. Alter your perception of perfection for reality. You must be honest about your abilities, the things you can do and how you can do them. Once you are honest with yourself, it is easier to appreciate your input and be more confident.

CBT Toolbox

Identifying Low Confidence Triggers

My confidence is lowest at these moments:

1.

2.

3.

4.

5.

6.

The following events have made me feel so low, and unable to do anything.

1.

2.

3.

4.

Identify Distorted Feelings

How do I feel when I am low on confidence?

1.

2.

3.

4.

When I am not confident, these are some of the things I prefer:

1.

2.

3.

4.

Because I wasn't feeling confident, I have avoided the following responsibilities:

1.

2.

3.

4.

List down some of the consequences you have endured as a result of low confidence:

1.

2.

3.

4.

Alternative Coping Skills

I believe I can change for the better, and turn my life around. Whenever I am not feeling confident enough, I will try the following:

1.

2.

3.

4.

Challenge the Distorted Thoughts

Lack of confidence should not hold you back. It is possible to replace the distorted thoughts with logical responses.

Distortion: I will probably fail this interview

Logic: I have prepared so long for this. I will give it my best shot. I have polished on my communication skills since my last interview, and I know I am ready for this.

1. *Distortion:*

Logic:

2. *Distortion:*

Logic:

3. *Distortion:*

Logic:

4. *Distortion:*

Logic:

Chapter 7:
Dealing with Depression

Cognitive behavioral therapy can help you manage the negative thought process that might be making it difficult for you to overcome depression. Depression keeps you from enjoying the best there is in life. Constantly thinking about negative things will keep you depressed. According to scientists, people who struggle with depression do not do so for lack of positive thoughts but because they can hardly allow themselves to think about and feel such thoughts. With depression, the main behavioral change is that people find it difficult to do things, and so they do less and often withdraw from people (Greenberger & Padesky, 2015). The psychological process is referred to as dampening.

Dampening makes you suppress any positive thoughts and emotions. Emotional dampening makes you convince yourself that you do not deserve good things, you do not deserve happiness. Even when something good is happening, you are skeptical, knowing it will not last.

Why does this happen to you when you are depressed? What can you do about it? One possible explanation experts offer is that you give the negative voice in your head a lot of power. It evolves into a pessimistic defense mechanism. What starts as subtle skepticism manifests into a defeatist thought process because you are afraid of getting your hopes up.

No one wants to play the fool in any situation. In response to this fear, you dampen all positive thoughts to stay safe from disappointment. Unfortunately, disappointment is a part of life. Things will not always go your way.

Understanding Depression

One of the biggest struggles you might be having with depression is a sense of pessimism or negativity. Even when good things are happening, you do not trust that they will remain good for a long time. You worry that it is not real, or it will not last long.

It is okay to open up and feel the things you are feeling. It is only human that you do. However, they should not steal your life from you. You have a better life ahead of you, and depression cannot take that away from you. There is always a way out. Speak to someone. You best believe it, things do get better.

How Does CBT Help with Depression?

CBT is one of the most successful methods of dealing with depression. It is a gradual process where, with the help of your therapist, you define the behavior patterns you need to change. The idea here is to reach into the part of your brain that suppresses the positive thoughts and recalibrate it to enable you to enjoy the good thoughts.

While CBT is effective, you also have to do so much more on your own outside the therapy sessions. You need to make sure you are in an environment that fosters change instead of making things worse. Start with the people around you. There should be a concerted effort to help you ignite the positive thoughts in the brain and encourage new patterns. CBT helps to liberate you from negative thought processes.

CBT Techniques for Depression

Following successful studies, most scientists believe individuals who are battling depression barely succeed with self-study. Therefore, you should seek professional help for no less than six weeks. Your therapist will try to learn more about your case of depression, what makes it worse, and the things you have been through.

There are techniques that your therapist will recommend after understanding what triggers your depression. Here are some possible methods you might work with:

Identifying the Problem

First, your therapist will try to connect with you at a different level and try to get you to let them in. You should try to let them feel the pain you are feeling. Simple conversations with the therapist will help you achieve this milestone.

Where possible, you will be advised to keep a journal. By taking notes, it is easier to refer and make a note of your progress. Taking notes will also help the therapist identify what is making you depressed. With this figured out, you begin the journey to improving the problem.

A feeling of hopelessness is normal when you are depressed. You feel like things are at their worst and will probably not get any better. You will be advised to write down things that are bothering you, things you are worried about and want to change but, for some reason, you cannot.

Using the example of someone who is depressed because they feel alone or lonely, your therapist might recommend that you join a club that focuses on your interests or some other activity that will help you interact with people freely and more often. Such interactions should help you ease into interactions and open up to new experiences.

Dealing with Negative Thoughts

Since you have already figured out some things that are making you think negatively, the next step would be to counter those thoughts. Note down the negative thoughts that come to mind whenever something happens. These are the thoughts that you give power while suppressing the positive ones.

For each negative thought you can think of, write a positive statement that you believe can help you overcome it. By writing these thoughts down, they are easier to remember. Rehearse them and try to speak them to yourself whenever you are caught up in a situation where you cannot think positively.

Rehearsal is a repetitive process that will, in the long run, help you replace negative thoughts with positive thoughts. The brain becomes aware of a new line of thinking and the more you tell yourself these positive thoughts, the easier it will be to replace the negative ones.

Since it might not be easy coming up with the ideal positive thoughts, think about something that is not so far from the negative thoughts. Let's assume the first thing that comes to your mind is: "*I am not happy with this life. Things don't seem to be going my way.*"

An ideal positive thought would be: "*People struggle all the time, and my case is no different. I have been through bad times before, and this too shall pass.*"

The message you are getting from this statement is that happiness is a hills and valleys experience, and it is okay. It is also a form of encouragement, keeping you safe from disappointment.

Creating New Opportunities

The next step is to discuss ways of encouraging positive thoughts. Even when things are not going according to plan, try to find something positive in a bad situation. Say you walk into a room but you dislike the furniture arrangement or the window placement. Instead of dwelling on that, you can appreciate the color on the walls or the paintings.

One way of addressing this is to get a friend that can help you manage your excitement. This way, whenever they come across something you might like, they will let you know immediately and keep you excited. Sharing such experiences throughout the day will go a long way in helping you feel better and think positively.

Evaluate Your Days

At the end of the day, go back to your journal and revisit the events that happened. Visualize the things that made you feel good or you are thankful for. You can also share some of them online if you wish. By revisiting these thoughts, you are making good progress regarding creating new associations in your mind. These are new memories that the brain is getting used to and falling in love with. As you keep doing this, you start having a positive outlook and approach to life.

Embrace Disappointment

Things are not always going to go your way. Disappointment is a part of life, and you should accept that. The way you respond to such a situation will determine how fast you can move on. Your current challenges can be overcome. There is nothing wrong with grieving about a bad situation. It helps you overcome the challenge.

If you have just broken up with someone, it is okay to feel down. However, do not blame yourself for the breakup. Instead, accept that you wanted different things in life and that there is someone out there who will love you just the way you are and in ways no one has ever loved you before.

To embrace disappointment, learn to live within your means. Take each experience you go through as a learning process. Identify your mistakes and promise to correct them in the future. Make changes in your life because they make you feel better and will make you a better version of yourself. Do not make changes because someone wants you to make them or because it suits the narrative they wish for you. Negative thoughts might occur from time to time, and this is okay. You should focus on moving on and building a better future for yourself.

CBT Toolbox

Identifying Depression Triggers

My definition of depression involves:

1.

2.

3.

4.

I feel so depressed when this happens

1.

2.

3.

4.

These are some of the things that happen right before I feel so low:

1.

2.

3.

4.

Identify Distorted Feelings

These are some of the feelings that make me feel depressed:

1.

2.

3.

4.

Whenever I feel depressed, this is what I do:

1.

2.

3.

4.

Other things I have previously done in an attempt to cope with depression include:

1.

2.

3.

4.

As a result of depression, I have suffered the following consequences:

1.

2.

3.

4.

Alternative Coping Skills

I want to live a positive life. Instead of this negativity, I will try the following to help me manage depression better. The next time I am feeling so low, I will try the following:

1.

2.

3.

4.

Challenge the Distorted Thoughts

This is about conquering your fears. Depression holds you back. It makes you live a dull, dark life, afraid to let anyone in. We can win this, if we think rationally about the things that you are concerned about.

I will give you an example to get you going:

Distortion: I cannot move on from my breakup

Logic: Of course, I will miss the good times. It is okay

to feel sad and lonely. But, I am not alone. There are people around me who are so warm and kind to me. I should spend more time with them. I will develop better, happier relationships, because there is someone out there for me, someone who will love me just the way I am, and appreciate me.

1. *Distortion:*

Logic:

2. *Distortion:*

Logic:

3. *Distortion:*

Logic:

4. *Distortion:*

Logic:

Chapter 8: Improving Ineffective Communication Skills

Networking and communication skills are vital skills you must learn to succeed in life today. Opportunities are continuously available at the workplace, at home, in church, you name it. Whenever you engage in a social construct, you find yourself in need of the right communication skills. These determine how well you get along with the people in your environment.

At each stage in life, you encounter different groups of people. Some people come into your life and walk away, only for fate to make your paths cross again at some point. Lack of proper communication skills can make it difficult for you to reconnect with people you were once close to, especially after spending so many years away from them. This explains why you would find every reason not to attend a reunion party.

Professionally, networking has become an essential part of our careers. You are invited to events all the time, and you interact with lots of people. You must maintain a good image for your company and your brand. Always remember that your individual presence represents the image of your company, and you must learn how to espouse the goals, objectives, vision, and mission of your company in these engagements.

While this might be overwhelming, it is possible through CBT. One of the most important skills in communication is to understand the behavior of other people around you and healthily respond to them. Effective communication relies on proper listening and the appropriate consequential response to the message you receive.

If you do not listen properly, you will often fail to get important information. Other than that, problems will catch you unawares when they arise. Listening is an effective way of understanding people, understanding their view of the world through their words, and helps improve communication between you and them. Listening also enables you to nurture and foster healthy relationships, whether you are making new ones or rekindling old ones.

Understanding Ineffective Communication Skills

Worried you are not able to communicate properly with those around you? When this happens, you worry about being reprimanded or punished. Inability to communicate with people will leave you feeling vulnerable. You are afraid to express yourself for fear of what your audience will think about you or say.

What happens here is you try to personalize a lot of concerns that you should not be worrying about in the first place. It is okay to let things take their course. You need to get out of your cocoon and speak your mind. Do not discount the positives and focus more on the negatives because they will stick. You have a voice, you need to be heard. Besides, if you cannot speak up for yourself, no one ever will.

Psychology of Listening

People love to be appreciated. This is why they respond better to those who listen to them. Listening and understanding what someone is talking about is a sign of emotional intelligence. Fostering quality relationships with people around you will depend on how well you can listen and communicate with them. You can learn these skills.

You must also know that to listen, you have to be keen and focus on what someone is telling you. Try to avoid pseudo-listening, which happens when you can hear someone but you can barely understand what they are talking about. Chances are high that you have other ideas in mind keeping you distracted, such as:

- Passing time until your opportunity to speak comes up
- Seeking vulnerabilities in the other person's speech
- Pretending to listen so you are likable
- Pre-emptive listening, where you are only alert for specific information, but blocking out everything else that you hear
- Trying to find out whether you are getting the response you desire from your audience
- Looking for weak points in an argument that you can use to intimidate the audience

You might have experienced these distractions from time to time. You might think you are smart and sharp, but in the long run, someone who has effective communication skills will figure you out. Some people might call you out on your flaws.

Improving Your Communication Skills

To develop your communication skills, you need to examine yourself and identify the factors that are hindering your communication with those around you. You get used to most of these factors and barely notice them. These factors are the listening blocks.

People use listening blocks all the time, and they make it difficult to communicate effectively with their audience. Once you identify these blocks, you can take steps to change them and improve. Making even subtle changes will eventually help you learn to listen and engage your audience better.

Stop Reading Minds

Instead of listening to someone, you are busy trying to figure out what they feel or what they are thinking. The problem with mind reading is that you never listen to the conversation around you. Instead, you are only waiting for cues and clues. This form of mental filtration makes you assume the reactions and intentions of people you are engaging.

Drawing Comparisons

Another trait you need to change is making comparisons between the speaker and yourself. Comparisons divert your attention from the subject matter, and instead, you focus on mundane things like how attractive the person is, whether they are funny or not, whether you are better at what they are saying or doing than they are. Since you are too busy trying to measure up, you miss the important discussion going on.

Pre-Judging

Many people are guilty of this one. Instead of starting a conversation on a clean slate, you have already formed an opinion of the speaker, of their message and intentions. Pre-judgment happens especially for individuals you have interacted with earlier or read about. You will barely focus on the conversation they are having with you because you have already decided they are too stubborn to meet your needs, writing them off in the process. Unfortunately, even if every opinion you have about them is valid, this might be that rare occasion where they do something out of the ordinary and you miss it.

Strong Debates

How often do you listen to someone instead of arguing with them? Many people barely listen to you when you speak to them. Instead, they take the first few words you say and turn it into an argument. In so doing, the focus of the conversation will be looking for points you can use in an argument or points that can win you the discussion instead of getting the message in the conversation.

Having such arguments in a conversation stems from having strong opinions about yourself or your ideas, preferences, and beliefs. Therefore, anyone who mentions anything not in line with what you consider the norm will not have a relaxed conversation with you. You should learn to listen and let someone finish what they are saying. This gives you time to evaluate their content and then make up your mind before raising an argument.

Giving Advice

You might be the type of person who barely lets someone complete a sentence before interjecting with some words of advice or dropping suggestions. You always feel you have so much more to offer, and the more you keep this up, people will feel you do not consider their opinions.

The problem with this is that, over time, you only get to hear the words that someone speaks to you but miss the emotions in the conversation. Someone might be trying to open up to you about something they are passionate about, or a personal problem, but you dismiss them even before they get to the point of comfort.

This is a concern that is shared a lot between superiors and their juniors, and over time, people find it difficult to talk to you about their problems. However much you try to get them to open up and talk to you about their struggles, they already know you will dismiss them.

CBT Toolbox

The things that trigger ineffective communication are more often the same things that cause a strain in relationships. This simple exercise will help you understand your weaknesses, and learn to communicate well with others.

What Triggers Poor Communication?

This is what I expect from effective communication:

1.

2.

3.

4.

These are some of the things that I feel prevent me from communicating well with others:

1.

2.

3.

4.

These are some of the people I struggle to communicate with:

1.

2.

3.

4.

I feel my communication problems are brought about by:

1.

2.

3.

4.

Identify Distorted Feelings

How do I feel when I am struggling to communicate effectively?

1.

2.

3.

4.

When I realize I cannot communicate with someone, these are my avoidance techniques:

1.

2.

3.

4.

List down some of the consequences you have endured as a result of poor communication:

1.

2.

3.

4.

Alternative Coping Skills

The following are some communication cues I want to practice and try each time I am communicating with someone:

1.

2.

3.

4.

Challenge the Distorted Thoughts

When you are unable to communicate with someone, you form opinions about them, and after a while, the opinions stick, and influence your communication with them henceforth. Most of these opinions are not true. Try to counter them with logic

I will give you an example to get you going:

Distortion: This is the most stupid employee ever. He never understands anything I say.

Logic: Maybe they have a hearing problem? What if I ask him why he never seems to understand me? Is he afraid of me? Am I overbearing? I think I should sit down with him at a comfortable time so we talk about it.

1. *Distortion:*

Logic:

2. Distortion:

Logic:

3. Distortion:

Logic:

4. Distortion:

Logic:

Conclusion

Having gone through this book, I hope you have learned a lot and made the first step toward progress. One of the most important things about changing for the better is to accept that you need help. This realization causes you to make a move and ask for help.

Asking for help is not a sign of weakness but a show of how strong you are. You are strong enough to realize you need someone to hold your hand and help you get back on the right path. We are social beings, and, as such, we exist in an environment with different social constructs.

How you interact with people in these circles will determine whether you get opportunities or not. Using these opportunities will decide whether you succeed in life. More often, the only thing that is holding you back is yourself.

CBT is about you. It is about helping you examine yourself and addressing the flaws you notice. Do not be afraid and do not shy away. You must also face your fears and conquer them. The days when you used to run away from your fears are long gone. Face them head on and rejoice in your triumphs.

Anxiety and depression have taken a toll on so many people. From celebrities to friends and family members, you have probably lost someone to depression. You will not give up. You will not give in.

You can fight. You can be a better you today than you were yesterday. You must believe in yourself because by so doing, people around you will see the same and believe in you too. Show them how awesome you are. Be the leader you were meant to be.

Remember, going to therapy does not necessarily mean you are sick, or an outcast. Going to therapy means you accept your flaws and that you are trying to correct them. You have noticed a weakness that you want to turn into a strength.

Once you overcome your adversities, nothing will hold you back.

ONE LAST THING

Reviews are one of the most important factors in a book's success.

Even if you are a bestselling author, your new book's fate – which you have toiled on for years – is in the hands of those few readers who take a minute to express their opinion of the book.

This one thing can be the difference between success and failure.

It would mean so much to me if you would take a moment to visit the page of this book (or any of my other titles) on Amazon.com and place a review. Or, if you don't wish to write a review, you can still help by simply voting Helpful or Unhelpful (or Thumbs up or Down) to the top 10 or so reviews.

As always, please feel free to leave an honest review, whether positive or negative.

Thank you!

Jeremy Crown

Made in the USA
Monee, IL
06 May 2021